Chefs
Community Workers

by Patricia Ryon Quiri

Content Adviser: Chef Wayne Almquist,
The Culinary Institute of America

Reading Adviser: Dr. Linda D. Labbo,
Department of Reading Education, College of Education,
The University of Georgia

COMPASS POINT BOOKS

Minneapolis, Minnesota

For my three sons—Rob, Brad, and C.J. I love to cook for you. Love, Mom

Special thanks to Executive Chef Tim Tighe and his sous chef, Larry Truitt, of East Lake Woodlands Country Club in Oldsmar, Florida

Compass Point Books
3109 West 50th Street, #115
Minneapolis, MN 55410

Visit Compass Point Books on the Internet at *www.compasspointbooks.com* or e-mail your request to *custserv@compasspointbooks.com*

Photographs ©:

FPG International/Richard Nowitz, cover; FPG International/Paul Avis, 4; FPG International/Art Montes De Oca, 6; Leslie O'Shaughnessy, 7; Unicorn Stock Photos/Jeff Greenberg, 8; Photo Network/Mark Sherman, 9; International Stock/Dusty Willison, 10; FPG International/Richard Nowitz, 11; Photo Network/Jeff Greenberg, 12; Unicorn Stock Photos/Jeff Greenberg, 13; Unicorn Stock Photos/ Jeff Greenberg, 14; FPG International/Jose Luis Banus, 15; FPG International/Suzanne Murphy-Larronde, 16; FPG International/ Arthur Tilley, 17; International Stock/Jonathan E. Pite, 18; International Stock/ Julian Cotton, 19; International Stock/George Ancona, 20; Photo Network, 21; FPG International/Ron Chapple, 22; Visuals Unlimited/ Jeff Greenberg, 23; Unicorn Stock Photos/Jeff Greenberg, 24; FPG International/ Arthur Tilley, 25; Leslie O'Shaughnessy, 26; International Stock/ Charlie Westerman, 27.

Editors: E. Russell Primm and Emily J. Dolbear
Photo Researcher: Svetlana Zhurkina
Photo Selector: Linda S. Koutris
Design: Bradfordesign, Inc

Library of Congress Cataloging-in-Publication Data

Quiri, Patricia Ryon.
   Chefs / by Patricia Ryon Quiri.
      p. cm. — (Community workers)
   Includes bibliographical references and index.
   Summary: Briefly describes the job of chef, including duties, artistry, and contribution to community.
      ISBN 0-7565-0007-9 (hardcover)
      ISBN 0-7565-1187-9 (paperback)
            1. Cooks—Juvenile literature. [1. Cooks. 2. Occupations.] I. Title. II. Series.
   TX652.5 .Q57 2000
   641.5'023—dc21   00-008619

Table of Contents

What Do Chefs Do?

A **chef** is the chief cook in a restaurant or hotel. The word *chef* comes from the French language. It is short for *chef de cuisine*, meaning "head of the kitchen."

◀ Chefs in the kitchen

A chef has many things to do. After planning the **menu**, he or she orders fresh bread, vegetables, fish, and meat every morning. Then the chef prepares the food and helps the other workers. A chef must make sure everything runs smoothly in the kitchen.

◀ A chef checks a produce delivery.

A chef and his assistant ▶ prepare a fruit tray.

What Tools and Equipment Do They Use?

In the kitchen, chefs have tools for making food for many people. Chefs and their helpers use special tools for peeling, slicing, mixing, and grinding. They also use ovens, grills, broilers, roasters, and steam kettles. Even the dishwashers are large!

◀ Chopping and preparing food in the kitchen

Chefs use a ▶ large mixer.

How Do Chefs Help?

Chefs make people happy. They feed tasty meals to hungry **customers**. They also make the food look pretty. Chefs work hard to please their customers and the **community**.

◀ A chef talks to a diner.

A chef tries to create a beautiful table. ▶

Where Do They Work?

Chefs work in many places. They cook in restaurants, hotels, and cafeterias. They also feed people in places such as airplanes, trains, hospitals, and schools.

◀ A chef cooks eggs in a restaurant.

A restaurant on a train ▶

Who Do They Work With?

Chefs have many helpers, including a **sous-chef**. *Sous-chef* is a French word meaning "assistant chef." The sous-chef prepares hot foods, such as gravies, vegetables, and pastas. The **pantry** cook is in charge of cold foods, such as salads, fruits, and cheeses. Fry cooks, vegetable cooks, and pastry cooks also help the chef.

A sous-chef cooks pasta.

A pastry chef decorates a cake.

What Do They Wear?

Chefs usually wear a white jacket, checkered pants, and a tall white hat. There are 100 folds in the chef's hat. Each fold represents a special way in which eggs can be served.

◄ A chef wears a tall hat and apron while he cooks outside.

A chef wearing a different kind of hat ►

What Training Does It Take?

It takes hard work to become a chef. Some chefs begin as a kitchen helper or cook's helper. They must finish high school. Some chefs also go to cooking school. There they learn how to plan menus, keep things clean, and manage the kitchen.

◀ A chef teaches students at a cooking school.

Students learn ▶ how to use a whisk properly.

What Skills Do They Need?

A restaurant kitchen is a busy, noisy place. Chefs must be able to work well with others and stand on their feet all day. They should also be **artistic** and like details.

◀ A busy kitchen

A beautiful table ▶
filled with food

What Problems Do They Face?

Chefs work long hours. Some chefs, such as bakers, begin work very early in the morning. Many chefs work at night, on weekends, and during holidays. Kitchens can also be very hot and dangerous places.

◀ A baker admires his work

Preparing food in ▶
a large kitchen

Would You Like to Be a Chef?

Do you like making up your own recipes? Maybe you would like to be a chef someday. You can prepare now. At home, ask to help in the kitchen. Read cookbooks and cooking magazines. When you are older, you might want to work in a restaurant as a food server.

◀ Cooking Mexican food at home

A teenaged server takes a customer's order. ▶

A Chef's Tools and Clothes

hat

jacket

pan

spatula

In the Kitchen

ingredients

pots

spoon

stove

pan

oven

A Chef's Day

Early morning
- The chef arrives at the restaurant early in the morning First, she plans the menu for the day.
- She also checks that the food in the kitchen is fresh.
- Next, she places orders for meat, fish, and vegetables.

Noon
- The chef shows a new kitchen helper how to chop vegetables.
- When the food arrives, the chef checks to make sure it is fresh and the right amount.

Afternoon
- The chef tries out a new fish recipe.
- The chef tells the servers about the evening's menu so they can describe it to customers.

Evening
- After taking a fresh piece of fish off the grill, the chef arranges it on the plate to look beautiful.
- During the busy meal hours, the chef visits the dining room to see if the customers like the new recipe.

Night
- After the restaurant is empty, the chef makes sure that the staff has left the kitchen clean and tidy.
- Exhausted, the chef heads home late at night.

Glossary

artistic—being creative about the way things look

chef—head of the kitchen

community—the people who live, work, play, and go to school in a certain area

customers—people who go to a restaurant for a meal

menu—a list of meals

pantry—a room where cold foods such as salads, fruits, and cheeses are kept

sous-chef—the chef's assistant who prepares hot foods such as gravies, vegetables, and pastas

Did You Know?

- The chef usually wears the tallest hat in the kitchen.

- About 3.4 million people work as cooks, chefs, and bakers in the United States.

- Americans spent more than $336.4 billion eating in restaurants in 1998.

- About 50 billion meals are eaten in U.S. schools, restaurants, and cafeterias every year.

Want to Know More?

At the Library

Duvall, Jill D., and Lili Duvall (photographer). *Chef Ki Is Serving Dinner!* Danbury Conn.: Children's Press, 1997.

Kalman, Bobbie. *The Kitchen*. New York: Crabtree Publishing Company, 1993.

Tames, Richard. *Food: Feasts, Cooks and Kitchens*. New York: Franklin Watts, 1994.

On the Web

The Culinary Institute of America

http://www.ciachef.edu/

To explore one of the most respected cooking schools in the world

Kids: Kings in the Kitchen

http://www.scoreone.com/kids_kitchen/

To try new recipes and share recipes with other kids

Through the Mail

American Culinary Federation, Inc.

10 San Bartola Drive

St. Augustine, FL 32086

For information about becoming a chef

On the Road

The Culinary Institute of America

433 Albany Post Road

Hyde Park, NY 12538-1499

800/285-4627

http://www.ciachef.edu/

To see students learning to be chefs and eat a delicious meal

Index

About the Author

Patricia Ryon Quiri lives in Palm Harbor, Florida, with her husband, Bob, and their three sons. She has a bachelor's degree in elementary education from Alfred University in upstate New York. She currently teaches second grade in the Pinellas County school system. Patricia Ryon Quíri is the author of twenty-one children's books.